CHAMPIONS OF PRAYER

CHAMPIONS OF PRAYER

RAISING UP AN ARMY OF FIRE

"Join the Ranks"

---but the people who know their God shall stand firm and take action- Daniel 11:32

PROPHETESS ANGEL ROBERTS

Copyright © 2025 Angel Roberts All rights reserved. No part of this publication may be reproduced, stored, or transmitted in any form without prior written permission of the author, except in brief quotations used in critical articles or reviews.

Published in the United States of America.

Scripture quotations are taken from various translations of the Holy Bible (e.g., KJV, NKJV, ESV, NIV) and are used with respect and acknowledgment of their respective publishers.

First Edition — 2025

ISBN: 979-8-9939161-0-1

DEDICATION

To my beloved mother, **Prophetess Bessie M. Spigner**, who has lived a life wholly dedicated to prayer, fasting, the study of God's Word, and the declaration of His truth.

Thank you for being a steadfast woman of faith who walks in obedience, shares the *rhema* word from Heaven, prophetic dreams, and divine insights.

Your legacy of faith continues through every *Champion of Prayer* rising in this generation.

I honor your life, your calling, and your unwavering devotion to the Kingdom of God. Thank you for raising up an army for God!

CONTENTS

Foreword V
Champions Of Prayer Are Champions Of Faith 1
Champion Your Faith 6
Completely Surrender To The Holy Spirit 11
The Hall Of Faith. Will You Join The Ranks? 18
Prayer Warriors Of The Bible Were World Changers 23
Rise To The Challenge, Stand In The Gap 28
We Are The Next Move Of God 34
Chosen, Called, And Anointed To Win 39
Your Words Have Power 44
Champion Your Prayer Life 49
Today Is The Day Of War Power — Not Willpower 56
I'm A No Name, Coming In His Name 61
End-Time Church — The Battering Ram 68
Volunteers In The Day Of Power 73
The Army Of Fire 80
Arise Church. The Time Is Now 91
Final Prayer: Lord, I Arise 98
Appendix: Declarations Of A Champion And Prayers 102
Conclusion 117
This Is A Call To Champion Your Prayer Life 117

FOREWORD

An End-Time Charge: Be an Army All by Yourself

Believers who follow the way of Christ are the Church of the Living God. In *Matthew 16:18*, Jesus said, "Thou art Peter, and upon this rock I will build my church, and the gates of hell shall not prevail against it."

We are the end-time remnant church. Church, it's time to get militant and vigilant in our faith walk with God! It's time to operate in the authority and power given to us, to bring Heaven to bear upon the earth.

"And from the days of John the Baptist until now, the Kingdom of Heaven suffereth violence, and the violent take it by force." — Matthew 11:12

The Lord told me to tell you: *You plus God are an unstoppable army!*

David was a one-person army. Scripture says, "He arose, and smote the Philistines." As the Church, that same power of God is available to you. Jesus said, *"Behold, I give you power..."* Are you willing to stand alone and fight?

We often want God to do everything, but He demands that each of us partner with Heaven to slay our enemies. You must be willing to fight for Heaven to invade the earth on your behalf, even if no one else goes with you.

Don't wait to see who else is fighting the good fight of faith; *you fight! You stand! You champion Heaven's cause!* God has called you! You must answer the call to *pray without ceasing!*

Rhema: Champions of Prayer Have Mastered the Secret Place

You must answer the call to the Secret Place. Your secret time with God is where battles are fought and won. It's in the Secret Place of Prayer that you build a deep relationship with God—one that strengthens your faith, provides divine guidance, and equips you for public life and ministry.

Champions of Prayer master the Secret Place! Why? Because *prayer births faith!*

When you learn to press in, your faith will rise like fire in your heart.

In 1 Samuel 1:12-15, Hannah prayed with such desperation that Eli the priest thought she was drunk. Yet that prayer birthed Samuel, the prophet who would anoint kings.

Champions of faith are first *Champions of Prayer*. Hannah prayed, and God moved. Faith is the bridge between your prayer and His answer.

Rise above the weariness and lift your voice, pray until the chains of discouragement fall away. Pray until your faith becomes a living power!

> *"This is the victory that has overcome the world—even our faith."— 1 John 5:4*

When prayer and faith join hands, the impossible becomes possible!

> *In Mark 9:23, Jesus said, "If you can believe, all things are possible to him who believes.*

1

CHAMPIONS OF PRAYER ARE CHAMPIONS OF FAITH

"But in all these things we are more than conquerors through Him who loved us."- Romans 8:37

God is raising up a bold Church filled with fire baptized intercessors, prayer warriors, faith filled leaders, and spiritual generals who know how to prevail in prayer, believe God without wavering, stand their ground when no one else will, and refuse to accept no for an answer. If God said it, I believe it, and I will pray until Heaven invades the earth on our behalf.

Being a Champion of Prayer is the same as being a Champion of Faith. The two cannot be separated because a praying church is a powerful church.

A true Champion of Faith does not only speak faith. They live it.

"Faith without works is dead."- James 2:26

Champions stand firm when the winds blow. They decree and declare the Word of God when the enemy roars. They rise to the challenge when others fall away.

"I have fought the good fight. I have finished the race. I have kept the faith."- 2 Timothy 4:7

When things are difficult and the way forward is unclear, Champions of Prayer continue to persevere because they know that God is faithful.

They walk in the footsteps of Jesus, who is the Author and Finisher of our faith. Jesus endured the cross because of the joy set before Him and through His victory purchased our salvation, healing, and deliverance. He is the greatest Champion of Faith.

"I can do all things through Christ who strengthens me." - Philippians 4:13

The strength of a Champion of Prayer does not come from titles or positions. It comes from intimacy with God, time spent in His Word, and obedience to His voice.

"They that wait upon the Lord shall renew their strength. They shall mount up with wings as eagles. They shall run and not grow weary. They shall walk and not faint."- Isaiah 40:31

The presence of the Lord fills the Champion with supernatural strength to rise and soar above life's tests and trials.

When your faith is tested, run into His presence.

When you feel depleted, run into His presence.

When everything comes at you at once, run into His presence.

When you face the unthinkable and the unimaginable, run into His presence.

"Times of refreshing come from the presence of the Lord." - Acts 3:19

Be refreshed. Be renewed. Be restored.

Declare This Now. I Decree and Declare

- I am the Church of the Living God. The gates of hell shall not prevail against me.

- I rise as a Champion of Prayer and a Champion of Faith.

- I will not shrink back. I will not faint. I will not retreat.

- I stand in the power and authority given to me through Jesus Christ.

- I partner with Heaven to overthrow every work of darkness.

I declare

- I am bold, militant, and vigilant in my walk of faith.

- I fight the good fight of faith and take the Kingdom by force.

- My prayer life is a weapon of fire and divine power.

- I stand like David and I rise to defeat every giant in my path.

- I will not wait for others to fight. I fight. I stand. I carry out the purpose of Heaven on the earth.

- I abide in the Secret Place where battles are won and where faith is born.

- I speak the Word of God with authority and divine strength.

- I am an overcomer and more than a conqueror, through Christ Who loves me.

- My faith is alive, active, and unshakable.

- I will pray until Heaven invades the earth.

- I will not be silenced. I will not step back.

- The fire of God strengthens me. The Spirit of God leads me. The power of God flows through me.

- I am called. I am chosen. I am anointed.

- I am equipped to shake nations through prayer and faith.

- I rise in the power of the Holy Spirit to reveal His glory in the earth.

I am a Champion of Prayer.

I am a Champion of Faith.

I am part of the unstoppable army of the Living God.

Prayer. Lord, Make Me a Champion of Faith

Lord, in the time of trouble, strengthen my heart to believe Your Word. Fill my mind with Your truth and fill my mouth with Your Word until Heaven rules the outcome. I decree and declare that I am a Champion of Prayer and a Champion of Faith. Let Your boldness rise in me, for the righteous are as bold as a lion. Make me fearless in the face of every trial as I move in the power of Your Spirit. Empower me to trust You, to keep my eyes on You, to walk with You, and to stand on Your Word no matter the cost.

In the mighty Name of Jesus, Amen.

2

CHAMPION YOUR FAITH

Champions are not made on platforms or stages. They are made in the prayer closet. Champions do not rise from talent alone, but from discipline, persistence, and faith in God. Prayer is the training ground, the gym of the spirit. I often say that prayer is where we press weights in the Holy Spirit. You cannot become a heavyweight in the Kingdom without prayer. Without prayer, faith grows weak. With prayer, faith is sharpened like a sword. Prayer builds faith, and faith fuels endurance. Champions cannot skip their training ground. They must embrace it in order to win.

> *"I have fought the good fight, I have finished the race, I have kept the faith."- 2 Timothy 4:7*

Faith is not passive. It is not only something you have but something you do. It requires active and obedient action rather than intellectual belief or silent waiting. Faith is not quiet. When you truly believe God, you are compelled to speak, aligning your words with your beliefs and giving your faith a voice in your life.

Faith is a force. It is a spiritual power that lives in the spirit of every believer. Faith is a fight that Champions win.

To champion your faith means you rise above fear, unbelief, and compromise. You stand with unwavering conviction no matter who stands with you or against you. Champions of Prayer are Champions of Faith because they have learned to believe God when everything looks impossible and to speak life when everything looks dead.

> "Faith is the assurance of things hoped for, the conviction of things not seen."- Hebrews 11:1

Faith is your spiritual backbone. You will not bend and you will not break. Faith allows you to speak with boldness, act in obedience, and stand in the middle of the storm. Prayer may not change the storm around you, but it will silence the storm within you.

Fight the Good Fight of Faith

Champions do not wait for perfect conditions, and they do not waver when life becomes difficult. Champions war with the Word. They wage warfare in prayer. They pray until walls fall, chains break, and strongholds collapse.

To walk by faith means you refuse to be ruled by what you see or feel. The only thing that moves a Champion is the Word of God.

> *"We walk by faith, not by sight."- 2 Corinthians 5:7*

Just as athletes remain persistent in training, Champions of Prayer refuse to be discouraged. They continue to fight the good fight of faith through consistent, bold, and unrelenting prayer.

God never promised the road would be easy, but He did promise victory. If God has declared that you are more than a conqueror, then you must believe it, speak it, and live it.

God Is Raising an Army with Bold Faith in a Lukewarm World

The world is full of complacent Christians, yet Champions of Prayer are dangerous and on fire. They are not ashamed of the Gospel and they are not intimidated by culture. Champions are filled with holy boldness. Their courage does not come from emotion but from the Spirit of God. This divine courage shapes their actions, attitudes, and momentum as they prevail in prayer.

> *"If God is for us, who can be against us?" - Romans 8:31*

Jesus is coming soon, and I believe we are the remnant He has chosen to usher Him in. We are the Church of the Living God and the enemy is doing everything possible to stop us, but this is not the time to shrink back. This is the time to move forward in faith. You do not have to feel qualified. Heaven has authorized and empowered you to raise your voice, walk in power, and declare the Word of God over your life, your family, your ministry, your business, your city, your territory, and your nation.

Your Faith Will Be Tested

"The testing of your faith produces perseverance." - James 1:3

Every Champion has scars. These scars are proof that you fought, endured, and overcame.

God allows your faith to be tested not to destroy you but to develop you. Just as a muscle grows through resistance, your faith grows stronger through testing. Your authority, endurance, and spiritual stamina are built in battle. God strengthens your backbone until it becomes like steel. You will not bend. You will not break. You will not be fragile. You will be fortified and resolute.

Declare This Now

- I am a Champion of Faith.
- I do not speak the problem. I decree and declare the solution.
- I am not moved by what I see. I am motivated by what God says.
- I believe God even when the outcome appears impossible.
- My faith is strong, growing, unmoving, and unshakable.
- I am bold, fearless, and full of the power of the Holy Spirit.

Prayer: Lord, Strengthen My Faith

Lord, I thank You for the gift of faith. Today, I choose to walk in boldness and refuse to back down from the attacks of the enemy. Make me a Champion who believes Your Word no matter what I face. I rebuke fear, doubt, and every deception of the enemy. Let every lying voice fail, and let Your truth prevail. Let my life be a testimony of obedience and victorious faith. In the mighty Name of Jesus, Amen.

3

COMPLETELY SURRENDER TO THE HOLY SPIRIT

"Walk by the Spirit and you will not gratify the desires of the flesh."- Galatians 5:16

To be a true Champion of Faith, you must learn to walk in spiritual self-control. This does not come by suppressing the flesh with human effort but by yielding completely to the Holy Spirit.

This is not partial surrender and it is not occasional obedience. This is complete submission to the Spirit's influence, guidance, and empowerment every day and in every area of your life.

Declaration: I do not live by the flesh. I walk by the Spirit. I give the Holy Spirit full control of my life.

Dying Daily: The Secret to Power

The Apostle Paul gave us a key to consistent victory.

"I die daily."- 1 Corinthians 15:31 (KJV)

Although Paul faced real danger every day, this statement reveals a spiritual discipline. A Champion of Faith must crucify the desires of the flesh and choose a consecrated lifestyle.

Bold Insight: Victory in the Spirit begins with the death of the flesh.

This daily surrender means choosing God's will over your comfort, cravings, emotions, and convenience. You do not allow the flesh to lead the way. You allow the Spirit to reign.

Faith Requires Discipline

"In a race everyone runs, but only one person gets first prize. So, run your race to win... I fight to win... I train my body to do what it should — not what it wants." — 1 Corinthians 9:24–27 (TLB, paraphrased)

A Champion of Faith is not soft, lazy, or aimless. They are trained, focused, and disciplined. They submit their body, thoughts, and habits to the will of God. They live like warriors who are preparing to win.

Empowering Reminder: My faith is not passive. My faith is disciplined, trained, and ready to conquer.

Prayer Fueled Power: Jesus Set the Example

Jesus walked in unmatched power and He gave us the blueprint. He modeled the rhythm of power through prayer. Luke tells us that Jesus often withdrew to lonely places to pray. He did not draw strength from the crowd. He drew strength from the secret place.

"And Jesus being full of the Holy Ghost returned from Jordan and was led by the Spirit into the wilderness for forty days. And when those days were ended, He returned in the power of the Spirit."- Luke 4:1-2, 14 (KJV)

If Jesus, the Son of God, needed fasting and prayer to walk in power, how much more do we?

Fasting, prayer, and declaring God's Word are not empty routines. They are invisible warfare.

Rhema: In order to get the supernatural, you must do the supernatural.

Your fasting, your prayer, and your declaration of God's Word are not empty routines. They are invisible warfare.

When you fast, heaven touches earth.

When you pray, the fire of heaven falls.

When you decree God's Word, angels are released.

> *"Is not this the fast that I have chosen to loose the bands of wickedness... Then shall your light break forth as the morning and the glory of the Lord shall be your reward."* Isaiah 58: 6, 8 – 9

Bold Truth: Your consecrated life makes a demand on heaven's armies to fight for you and win.

- When you fast, demons tremble.
- When you fast, angels shut the mouths of lions.
- When you fast, the power of heaven shifts the wind in your favor.

Spirit-led and Spirit-fueled: The secret to being a Champion of Faith is a consistent Spirit led and Spirit fueled consecrated life of prayer, fasting, and declaring the Word of the Lord.

The Holy Spirit Is Your Source of Power

The same Holy Spirit who raised Jesus from the dead is alive and active within every believer.

> "And if the Spirit of Him who raised Jesus from the dead is living in you, He who raised Christ will also give life to your mortal bodies because His Spirit lives in you." - Romans 8:11

> "His incomparably great power for us who believe is the same power God exerted when He raised Christ from the dead and seated Him at His right hand in heavenly places far above all rule and authority and every name that is invoked. God placed all things under His feet and appointed Him head over everything for the church which is His body." Ephesians 1:19-23

The exceeding greatness of His power is available to every believer. The same mighty power that raised Jesus is the same power that empowers the Church today.

The presence of the Holy Spirit within you is resurrection power. When you are filled with the Holy Spirit, you carry the power that conquered death. This power strengthens you to overcome everything that fights against the will of God for your life.

A Champion of Prayer understands this truth. The Holy Spirit is not optional. He is essential.

- He is your power source.
- He is your guide.
- He is your boldness.

- He is your voice.

Prophetic Declaration: I am led by the Spirit. I am filled with the Spirit. I am empowered by the Spirit to walk in victory.

You speak boldly because the righteous are as bold as a lion. You walk in authority because the Holy Spirit empowers you. You stand unshaken because no weapon formed against you will prosper.

And when your enemies rise, God will remove them.

Declare This Now

- I am not ruled by my flesh.
- I walk in the Spirit.
- I surrender daily.
- I pray without ceasing.
- I live a consecrated life through fasting, prayer, and declaring God's Word.
- I am led by the Spirit.
- I conquer through faith.
- My prayer life empowers my faith life.
- I am a Champion of Prayer and a Champion of Faith.

Prayer: Spiritual Surrender

Holy Spirit, I give You full control of my life. Teach me to die daily and crucify my flesh through fasting, prayer and the Word of God.

4

THE HALL OF FAITH. WILL YOU JOIN THE RANKS?

"And without faith it is impossible to please Him, for whoever would draw near to God must believe that He exists and that He rewards those who seek Him."- Hebrews 11:6

Heaven has a record. A roll call of warriors. A divine archive known as the Hall of Faith.

Heaven is not filled with celebrities, theologians, or influencers. It is filled with believers who dared to trust God in impossible situations. Men and women who had nothing but a Word from the Lord, and that was enough to move heaven on earth.

The world crowns talent. God crowns faith. Prayer is the road, and faith is the crown.

Heroes of the Hall of Faith

Hebrews chapter 11 reveals the names of the faithful. The ones who walked with God. The ones who obeyed when others mocked. The ones who moved when God said move, even when the instruction made no sense.

• Abel gave God his best and was counted righteous.

• Noah built an ark when there was no rain in sight.

• Abraham left everything to pursue a promise.

• Sarah believed in a miracle beyond her years.

• Joseph held to God's dream through betrayal and imprisonment.

• Moses chose God over the luxury of Egypt.

• Rahab risked her life to protect God's people.

• Gideon, Barak, Samson, and David conquered kingdoms, shut the mouths of lions, and defeated giants.

None of them was perfect, but they believed, obeyed, and trusted God. Their faith wrote history in heaven.

Will You Join the Ranks? Will Your Name Be Counted?

There is still room in the Hall of Faith. Will your name be written?

Faith is not reserved for the men and women in the Bible. It is a daily call to the Church to trust God radically.

Every time you choose obedience over self-will and faith over fear, you write your name in heaven's record.

Whether you preach to nations, take your city, minister to your community, or lead your family with faith, you are counted among the Champions.

When you choose to believe God for your healing, your family, your assignment, and your breakthrough, you are writing your story in faith. When you declare God's promises in the face of warfare, heaven takes notice.

God is actively searching the earth for hearts that are fully committed to Him so that He can show Himself strong.

> *"The eyes of the Lord range throughout the earth to strengthen those whose hearts are fully committed to Him."—— 2 Chronicles 16:9*

Champions Are Still Being Written

You are not here by accident. You were born for such a time as this. You were called, chosen, equipped, anointed, and appointed. Your name is known in heaven. You were born to believe, determined to conquer, and destined to secure heaven's victories.

> *"These were all commended for their faith, yet none of them received what had been promised, since God had planned something better for us..."* — Hebrews 11:39–40

When life becomes difficult, remember that God included you in the legacy of faith. He chose you to help write the next chapter of the Hall of Faith.

The question remains. Will you walk by faith and conquer your fear? Will you dare to trust God above all else?

Declare This Now

- Heaven knows my name.

- I walk in the footsteps of faith-filled heroes.

- I am bold, unwavering, and obedient to God's voice.

- I am counted in the Hall of Faith. I am faithful, loyal, and trusting in God.

- My legacy is faith. My language is faith. My lifestyle is faith.

Prayer. Lord, Count Me Among the Faithful

Father, I thank You for the testimony of the great cloud of witnesses. Let my life echo their legacy. Let my choices honor You. Help me to trust You when it is hard. Help me to obey when it is uncomfortable and to believe when it is unpopular. Count me among those who live by faith, finish strong, and finish well, in the mighty Name of Jesus, Amen.

5

PRAYER WARRIORS OF THE BIBLE WERE WORLD CHANGERS

"The effective, fervent prayer of a righteous man availeth much."-
James 5:16 (KJV)

Prayer is not a passive practice. It is a powerful and effective weapon. Prayer is heaven's legal invitation for God to intervene on the earth. When a righteous person prays, atmospheres shift. Prayer changes things.

In the Bible, prayer warriors were world changers. They did not pray pretty prayers. They prevailed, they travailed, they interceded, and they wept between the porch and the altar. Their prayers birthed nations, dismantled kingdoms, exposed enemies, healed the sick, raised the dead, and called fire from heaven.

Who Were These Warriors That Changed History On Their Knees

Let us walk among the Champions of Prayer from Scripture:

• Moses stood in the gap and turned away the wrath of God. Read Exodus 32:11-14

• Hannah prayed through bitterness and barrenness until God gave her a prophet.

• David prayed for his nation and wrote psalms of intercession and repentance.

• Daniel prayed fervently in the face of death.

• Deborah was a judge and prophetess whose prayers led to military victory.

• Elijah prayed, and the heavens closed. He prayed again, and the rain returned.

• Jesus often withdrew to pray, even all night. He showed us that power flows from intimacy with God.

• Paul prayed consistently for strength, for the churches, and for spiritual insight.

These warriors were not perfect, except for Jesus. They were consistent, persistent, surrendered, and relentless in prayer.

Today, God is Still Raising Up Prayer Warriors

Heaven is looking for intercessors. People who will stand in the gap, cry aloud, war in the Spirit, and declare the will of God in the earth. Have you answered the call to change history on your knees?

> *"And I sought for a man among them, that should make up the hedge, and stand in the gap before me for the land..." — Ezekiel 22:30*

Who will answer the call to intercession? There is a gap in your generation. There is a gap in your family. There is a gap in your nation. God is calling you to stand in that gap. I will speak more about standing in the gap in the next chapter.

One prayer warrior can shift an entire bloodline. One intercessor can call for justice and hold back judgment. One voice can call revival down from heaven.

Prayer is Power

The enemy fears praying believers more than preaching ones. Prayer disrupts the demonic. It invites God's glory to manifest. It binds the strongman and opens the heavens.

Prayer gives you divine intelligence, heavenly strategies, spiritual perception, and spiritual vision.

You do not have to be seen to be powerful. You must be intentional, consistent, and anointed.

Prayer is where the battle is fought and won. Prayer power is victory on your knees before you ever step onto the battlefield.

Declare This Now

• I am a prayer warrior.

• I exercise my authority and legislate from heaven.

• My prayers carry weight, power, and the divine backing of heaven.

• I intercede for my family, those connected to me, my generation, my city, and my nation.

• I am a Champion of Prayer. Hell cannot defeat me, and hell cannot stop me.

(I will speak more about standing in the gap in the next chapter.)

Prayer: Use Me from the Place of Prayer

Dearest Heavenly Father,

Teach me to pray as Jesus prayed, with spiritual clarity, power, passion, and purpose. Make me sensitive to the prompting of the Holy Spirit. Use my prayers to tear down strongholds and release Your will on earth. Let my voice be heard in heaven. Let my prayers birth revival. I yield my heart, my words, and my time to become a Champion of Prayer.

In Jesus' Mighty Name, Amen.

6

RISE TO THE CHALLENGE, STAND IN THE GAP

"I looked for someone among them who would build up the wall and stand before me in the gap on behalf of the land."- Ezekiel 22:30 (NIV)

There is a gap in your family.

There is a gap in your generation.

There is a gap in your nation.

And God is calling you to stand in it.

You do not need a platform. You do not need a pulpit. All you need is a posture, the posture of intercession.

In every generation, God looks for someone. One person. Someone who will stand in the place of prayer, speak His Word, and legislate His will. God has chosen you.

Activate Your Gap Standing Power

To stand in the gap means you place yourself between heaven and earth. Between judgment and mercy. Between the breach and the breakthrough. It means you are spiritually present when others are spiritually asleep. It means you take responsibility in prayer even when others are running from the battle.

It is not glamorous. It is glorious.

It is not loud. It is powerful.

It is not seen by men. Its power shakes the heavens.

You are called to be a watchman, a gatekeeper, and a spiritual warrior. Watchmen see in the Spirit, discern the times, and do not sleep while the enemy advances.

Like Nehemiah rebuilding the wall, they build with one hand and war with the other.

> *"I have posted watchmen on your walls, Jerusalem. They will never be silent day or night."* - Isaiah 62:6

Champions of Prayer will not be silent. They remind God of His promises to heal, save, deliver, and restore His people. They give Him no rest until His promises are fulfilled.

Declaration: I will not sit back in silence. I will rise in the Spirit and stand in the gap for my generation.

Intercession Is Invisible Warfare

Intercession is you exercising governmental authority. When you pray, you legislate heaven's will on earth. You block the enemy's access. You cancel demonic assignments. You break generational curses. You overturn decrees of death. You speak heaven's verdict over earth's chaos. You birth revival.

- Abraham stood in the gap for Sodom.

- Moses stood in the gap for Israel.

- Esther stood in the gap for her people.

- Jesus stood in the gap for the world.

> *"He ever liveth to make intercession."* - Hebrews 7:25

This is not passive praying. It is militant intercession. It is Kingdom governance. It is a spiritual disruption. Hell, trembles when intercessors take their place.

Intercessors Operate from a Position of Power

"And God raised us with Christ and seated us with Him in the heavenly realms in Christ Jesus." - Ephesians 2:6

You do not intercede from earth looking up. You pray from heaven, looking down. You are seated in a position of spiritual authority and superiority, above principalities, powers, and rulers of darkness.

When you stand in the gap, you are operating in Kingdom dominion.

A Call to the Watchmen

Do Not Let the Fire on Your Altar Go Out

Gap standers are fuel carriers.

They do not let the fire die.

They stir it.

They protect it.

They multiply it.

"The fire shall ever be burning upon the altar. It shall never go out." -Leviticus 6:13

This is not the time to sleep.

This is not the time to be distracted.

The Church must arise and take its post.

There are breaches in the wall. The enemy is coming for families, leaders, governments, and children. But God is sounding the alarm.

Who will rise?

Who will pray?

Who will stand in the gap?

You must say, Here I am, Lord. Send me.

Declare This Now

- I am a watchman on the wall.

- I stand in the gap for my generation.

- I intercede with authority, passion, and power.

- No weapon formed against my family, city, or nation will prosper.

- I am a Champion of Prayer. I am bold, alert, anointed, and unshakable. I will not be moved.

Prayer: I Will Stand in the Gap

Lord, awaken the watchman in me. Train my hands for war and my heart for intercession. Give me discernment to see, boldness to speak, and faith to declare. I take my place in prayer with fire in my belly and authority in my voice. May supernatural breakthroughs, divine protections, and revival fires be birthed through my obedience.

In Jesus' Mighty Name, Amen.

7

WE ARE THE NEXT MOVE OF GOD

"For the creation waits in eager expectation for the children of God to be revealed."-Romans 8:19 (NIV)

This world is groaning. The nations are shaking. Morality is crumbling. Evil is becoming bold. This is not the time to retreat. This is the moment for the Church to rise with prophetic insight and power.

We do not need another program. We need a move of God. We do not need celebrity Christianity. We need the fire of God's presence and the wind of His Spirit to fill pulpits, pews, classrooms, and street corners.

God is calling His Champions to pray, travail, decree, declare, and prepare for a Kingdom invasion. The world is not waiting for another political leader. The world is waiting for you. A blood bought, blood washed, fire baptized, glory carrying believer who will stand in the power of the Holy Spirit and say:

"Lord, let Your Kingdom come. Let Your will be done on earth as it is in heaven."

You have the power to call heaven to earth. You have the power to shift the direction of the wind. You have the power to silence the raging storm.

> *"You shall also decide and decree a thing, and it shall be established for you, and the light of God's favor shall shine upon your ways."- Job 22:28 AMPC*

You pray and usher in the next move of God. The power of the Holy Spirit is within you.

You Are the Next Revival

The move of God is not coming from the outside. It is being birthed from within. It is birthed in prayer and intercession.

While you pray for revival, remember that you are the revival. You are not only interceding for change. You are the change.

The same Spirit that raised Jesus from the dead lives in you. You are a mobile Ark of the Covenant. Wherever you go, heaven has permission to move. Hallelujah. You are the icebreaker. You are the flame thrower. You are the man of war. You are God's vessel of breakthrough.

Let the Winds of the Spirit Blow

"From the North to the South, from the East to the West, let the euroclydon winds of the Holy Spirit blow."

Cindy Trimm

We decree:

- A shaking in the heavens

- A purging in the pulpits

- A remnant rising from the ashes

- A bold and prophetic Church marching in power

We need a move of God in our country. We need a move of God in our churches, schools, cities, families, and governments. We need the winds of the Spirit to blow with supernatural force to root out, pull down, overthrow, and rebuild.

God is calling intercessors, priests, prophets, revivalists, and watchmen to rise and go. God is calling you to usher in His Glory.

Prophetic Declaration

We are the Church of the Living God, and no power in hell can stop us. We are the ekklesia, set apart for the Master's use. We are the Church of the Living God, armed for war, anointed and appointed to destroy the works of darkness.

> *"Upon this rock I will build My church, and the gates of hell shall not prevail against it."- Matthew 16:18*

In the days ahead, the light of God's glory will pierce the darkness through Champions of Prayer who have strengthened their faith. They know who they are, they know whose they are, and they know there is no power greater than the power of our God. We hold firm to the altar and embrace the power of His presence as we behold His Glory. Let the Church arise.

Declare This Now

- I am the next move of God

- The Spirit of the Lord is upon me, and I am anointed to shift nations

- I decree and declare the winds of revival will bring restoration, healing, health, provision, and salvation

- I decree and declare that heaven will invade my generation

- I have a voice in heaven that impacts the earth. I am a speaking spirit. I am steadfast, unmovable, unshakable, and unstoppable

Prayer: Lord, Let the Revival Begin with Me

Dearest Heavenly Father,

Let heaven invade the earth. Set Your Church on fire again. Shake everything that can be shaken. Loose us from every chain. Set us free so we can set the captive free. Let the anointing of the Breaker be released to bring divine disruption and a holy awakening. Let there be a great outpouring of the power of the Holy Spirit upon all flesh. Cause our sons and daughters to prophesy. Speak to and through every Dreamer. Raise Glory Carriers who will birth the next move of God. In Jesus' Mighty Name, Amen.

8

CHOSEN, CALLED, AND ANOINTED TO WIN

"But you are a chosen generation, a royal priesthood, a holy nation, His own special people, that you may proclaim the praises of Him who called you out of darkness into His marvelous light."- 1 Peter 2:9 (NKJV)

You are called. You were chosen. You are anointed to lead. God did not create you just to survive or blend in. He created you to rise and thrive in your generation as the Army of God, a Kingdom Voice, and a Glory Carrier.

The enemy attacks believers to convince them that they are not strong enough, bold enough, smart enough, or powerful enough to withstand his pressure. But there is a power inside you that no other power can overcome. Press deeper into the presence of God. God called you, equipped you, qualified you, and anointed you to win.

This Is the Hour of the Anointed Leader. You Must Be Oily

Many years ago, the Lord spoke these words;

"It is to the degree that you make yourself available to my power that you will see my power."

Are you available for God to use? It is not perfection that God looks for. It is availability.

Moses lacked confidence and struggled with speech.

Gideon was fearful and full of doubt.

David faced failure and scandal.

Esther was an orphan.

Jeremiah was young and felt inadequate.

Peter denied Jesus.

Paul persecuted believers.

But when the anointing came upon them, they became unstoppable. The oil of the Holy Spirit gives you the power to win.

"Not by might, not by power, but by my Spirit," says the Lord of hosts." - Zechariah 4:6

Your leadership is not based on personality or human connections. It is based on the call of heaven. It's the power of the Holy Spirit, the anointing on your life, that can do what natural talent and charisma cannot do.

Challenge: Step Into Leadership with Fire

You are anointed to do the work of the Kingdom. You are anointed to:

- Cast out devils

- Lay hands on the sick

- Speak with heavenly authority

- Establish Kingdom order

- Break generational curses

- Shift atmospheres

- Advance the Kingdom of God in the earth

You are not only a believer. You are a Kingdom influence, a carrier of power, an atmosphere shifter, and a vessel fit for the Master's use.

You carry a mantle to lead and take territory for the Kingdom of God. Wherever God places you, He will build a path of power ahead of you as you represent Him. Rise and reclaim your home, your children, your city, your business, and your ministry.

Anointed Ones Are a Danger to the Agenda of Hell

The devil is not afraid of titles. He is scared of the anointed ones.

You have gone through fire for a purpose. Trials train you. Testings stretch your faith. Warfare prepares you. Now is your moment to step into your God given position.

Let the fearful step aside. Let the weary rise again. Let the anointed and appointed take their rightful place.

You were chosen for this moment in history. You are called to lead. You are anointed to win.

Declare This Now

- I am called, chosen, anointed, and appointed by God
- I am anointed to lead

- The hand of the Lord is upon my life

- I walk in the supernatural favor, wisdom, and power of God

- I was born to conquer adversity, built to overcome obstacles, anointed to wage war and win, and appointed to advance the Kingdom of God

Prayer: Lord, I Accept the Call

Dearest Heavenly Father,

I say yes to Your call on my life. I surrender to the anointing and the assignment You have given me. Break every limitation. Silence every lie. Launch me into leadership with boldness. Give me clarity, courage, and divine confidence. Let the fire of the Holy Spirit empower me to lead with wisdom, humility, and breakthrough authority. I declare that I am called to lead, and I am anointed to win. In Jesus' Mighty Name. Amen.

9

YOUR WORDS HAVE POWER

"Death and life are in the power of the tongue. They that love it shall eat the fruit of it."- Proverbs 18:21 (KJV)

Your Tongue Is a Weapon

Your mouth is not only for communication. It is a spiritual weapon. God did not create the world with His hands. He created it with His words. Because you were made in His image, your words also create, shape, frame, tear down, build up and plant.

The enemy wants to silence your voice because he knows your voice carries the authority of heaven.

Champions of Prayer do not speak empty words. They speak power, purpose, and prophetic destiny into the atmosphere.

Your words are weapons.

Your words are keys.

Your words are containers of power that carry life or death, victory or defeat, breakthrough or bondage.

You Are Speaking Spirits. What You Say Shapes What You See

God created the universe by speaking. He said, "Let there be," and it was so. He created you in His image, which means you are a speaking spirit with the ability to shape reality through your words.

> *"Since we have the same spirit of faith according to what is written, 'I believed, and so I spoke,' we also believe, and so we also speak."* — 2 Corinthians 4:13

Champions of Prayer understand that declarations are not hype. They are heaven's strategy. When you speak God's truth, hell shakes, chains break, and angels are released.

Your Mouth Is a Gate. Heaven Moves at the Sound of Your Voice

God told Jeremiah:

> *"I have put my words in your mouth. I have set you over nations and kingdoms to uproot, pull down, destroy, overthrow, build, and plant."* - Jeremiah 1:9 - 10

Every time you open your mouth, you open a gate in the spirit realm.

• When you speak fear, you open the gate to torment

• When you speak doubt, you open the gate to delay

• When you speak faith, you open the gate to the power of heaven

• When you speak truth, you release the will of God into your world

Faith is never silent. Faith speaks. With every word you speak, you are either empowering heaven or empowering hell.

Align Your Mouth with the Word of God

Train your mouth to agree with heaven.

• Speak what God says, not what you feel

• Speak the outcome, not the obstacle

• Speak life, not limitation

• Speak breakthrough, not breakdown

Jesus did not talk about the storm. He spoke to the storm.

Elijah did not wish for fire. He declared it.

David did not describe Goliath. He prophesied his fall.

Stop describing what you are going through. Start declaring what God is bringing you into.

Decree It and It Shall Be Established

> *"You will decree a thing and it will be established for you. Light will shine on your ways." - Job 22:28 (NASB)*

When you decree the Word of God, you are issuing a ruling from the court of heaven. A decree is not a suggestion. It is an order backed by the full authority of God.

You have the authority to prophesy, rebuke, bless, declare, bind, and loose. Use that authority with boldness. You are not making suggestions. You are making rulings.

Angels respond to and act upon the Word of God.

Demons obey the Word of God.

Speak it boldly. Declare it consistently. Watch God confirm His Word with supernatural results.

Declare This Now

• My words carry power

• I am seated with Christ in heavenly places. I walk in divine power and kingdom purpose

• I uproot every lie. I destroy every curse. I remove every stronghold by the authority of God's Word. No weapon formed against me will prosper

• I speak breakthrough, healing, favor, and victory

• I plant the promises of God into my future through my words

Prayer: Lord, Guard My Mouth and Activate My Voice

Dearest Heavenly Father,

Thank You for the power You placed in my tongue.

Forgive me for using my words carelessly. Teach me to speak life. Train me to decree Your Word with boldness.

Let my declarations shift atmospheres, silence demons, and release divine outcomes. I declare that I am a Champion of Prayer and that my words are filled with the power of heaven. In Jesus' Mighty Name. Amen.

10

CHAMPION YOUR PRAYER LIFE

"Behold, I give you authority to trample on serpents and scorpions and over all the power of the enemy, and nothing shall by any means hurt you."- Luke 10:19 (NKJV)

Prayer Is the Place of Dominion

Prayer is not only a place of request. It is the place of rulership and authority.

When you pray, you are not begging. You are governing.

When you pray, you are not pleading as a slave. You are issuing decrees as a king.

Make this declaration:

I do not pray from earth to Heaven. I pray from Heaven to earth. I am seated with Christ, and I operate from the place of power.

"God raised us with Christ and seated us with Him in the heavenly realms in Christ Jesus."- Ephesians 2:6

You not only have access to God. You have access to His authority. The word authority is translated from the Greek word exousia. It means delegated power, the right to act, the right to command, and the ability to make things happen. It includes the power to overcome the enemy and the power to walk in victory.

Delegated power enables you to act.

As sons of God, we have the right, the ability, and the spiritual strength to stand against opposition and come out untouched.

To tap into the presence of God is to tap into His power. There is no separation between God and His power.

You were born to make things happen. You were born to rule and reign.

From the very beginning, God gave humankind dominion. Through Jesus Christ, that dominion has been restored to every believer who rises in prayer and walks in authority.

Champions of Prayer operate from a place of dominion. They use their authority to advance the Kingdom of God on earth.

You Have Access

See yourself seated in heavenly places with Christ Jesus.

You are not praying in order to win. You are praying from a position of victory.

You are not begging for access. You already have access.

This means:

- You are above every principality

- You are above every demonic interference

- You are above fear, confusion, sickness, and lack

When you pray, you govern from the throne room of God. You execute His decisions on the earth. Your dominion is activated in the secret place and revealed in the public place.

Prayer Is a Legal Act of Dominion

You are Heaven's special forces on earth. Your prayers carry legal authority.

- You declare healing and sickness must flee

- You declare peace, and chaos must bow

- You bind demons and they lose their grip

- You loose angels and they carry out assignments

- You open doors, and no man can shut them

"Whatever you bind on earth will be bound in Heaven. Whatever you loose on earth will be loosed in Heaven."- Matthew 18:18

Prayer is not only a spiritual practice. It is a governmental act. You are not pleading. You are reigning.

You were born to rule. You were born to reign. You were born to make things happen. The enemy knows it and tries to destroy you before you understand it.

Speak Like a King and Advance Like a Champion

You are more than a conqueror. You are the victor in this battle. You are not a victim.

Victims complain

Kings decree

Victims retreat

Champions advance

Wage a good warfare. Step into prayer as a kingdom representative. Stand in agreement with the will of God and declare it into manifestation.

You do not fight for dominion. You walk in the power of dominion. Christ holds supreme authority, and the church has been given the right to use it.

Your Authority Is Backed by the Throne room of Heaven

Jesus said,

> *"All authority has been given to Me." - Matthew 28:18*

> *"He is far above every ruler, authority, power, and dominion." - Ephesians 1:21*

> Jesus also said, *"I give you the keys of the kingdom of heaven." - Matthew 16:19*

You have been authorized and deputized by Heaven to enforce God's will and interrupt the plans of hell.

The blood of Jesus is your badge.

The Word of God is your weapon of power.

The Devil Respects God Given Authority

When you pray from the seat of dominion:

- Demons recognize your voice

- Strongholds weaken

- Generational curses break

- Prophetic atmospheres open

- Angelic activity increases

The devil does not fear church attendance. The devil fears the believer who champions their faith and knows who they are and where they sit.

You are that believer.

Declare This Now

- I am seated with Christ in heavenly places

- I rule and reign through prayer

- I do not beg. I legislate. I do not plead. I declare

- Every time I pray, Heaven moves and hell shakes

- I walk in dominion and I enforce the will of God on earth

Champions of Prayer carry the weight of the Kingdom within them.

Prayer: Teach Me to Reign and Rule in Prayer

Dearest Heavenly Father,

I thank You that through Christ I am seated in heavenly places. I receive the mantle of dominion authority.

Teach me to pray with power, to speak with authority, and to wage war with boldness.

Let my intercession shape nations and influence atmospheres. Let my words bring Heaven to earth.

I declare that I am not a victim. I am a victor. I walk in dominion.

I pray from the position of power.

I declare that I am a Champion of Prayer and I walk in authority.

In Jesus' Mighty Name, Amen.

11

TODAY IS THE DAY OF WAR POWER – NOT WILLPOWER

"'Not by might nor by power, but by my Spirit,' says the LORD Almighty." - Zechariah 4:6 (NIV)

The Difference Between Willpower and War Power

There is a spiritual war raging in the unseen realm, and it cannot be won with willpower alone.

Willpower is human effort.

War Power is Holy Ghost power.

Willpower relies on flesh.

War Power draws from the Spirit.

Bold Declaration: *Today is not the day for willpower, it's the day for war power!*

You cannot defeat demonic strategies with fleshly effort. You cannot overcome principalities with motivational quotes. You need the Spirit of God rising within you with fire, boldness, and power.

Superimpose War Power Over Willpower

To walk in dominion, you must superimpose the power of the Spirit over the desires of the flesh. This happens through:

- Cultivating your prayer time

- Incorporating intentional seasons of fasting

- Increasing your study of the word

- Meditating on the truth of Scripture

- Declaring the promises of God

When you do these things, the Holy Spirit disarms temptation, shuts down negative thoughts, and empowers you to overcome what once defeated you.

Prophetic Insight: *You were never meant to fight alone; the Spirit of the Lord is your war strategy!*

Authority That Crushes the Enemy

Jesus did not leave you powerless — He armed you with authority.

> *"Behold, I give unto you power to tread on serpents and scorpions, and over all the power of the enemy..." - Luke 10:19 (KJV)*

You were given the right to walk on the enemy, not wrestle endlessly with him.

When you pray in the Spirit, speak the word, and walk in consecration, you enforce the victory Christ already won.

> *"And having spoiled principalities and powers, he made a shew of them openly..." - Colossians 2:15 (KJV)*

The war is already won, now you execute that victory on earth.

Win the War in Your Mind — Walk in Power

> *"Greater is He that is in you than he that is in the world." - 1 John 4:4*

The battle begins in the mind but is won in the Spirit.

The enemy whispers lies, the flesh makes excuses, but the Spirit brings truth, power, and breakthrough.

You must put your foot down and declare:

Bold Statement:

I will not be ruled by my emotions, habits, or fears.

I live by the Spirit. I walk in the Spirit.

I move in war power — not willpower!

Prayer-Fueled Domination

Champions of Prayer do not live in cycles of defeat.

Champions of Prayer crucify the flesh and dominate in the Spirit.

You are not fighting *for* victory — you are fighting *from* victory.

Bold Statement: *I am not surviving — I'm advancing!*

I am not trying — I am triumphing!

Declare This Now:

- I choose war power over willpower.

- I do not fight in my flesh — I fight in the Spirit.

- I am filled with the Holy Ghost war power.

- I fast. I pray. I decree. I conquer.

- Temptation has no power over me.

- The Spirit shuts down every lie and lifts me into victory.

- I dominate in the Spirit and crucify my flesh.

- I am a Champion of Prayer, and I walk in war power — not willpower!

Prayer: Ignite War Power Within Me

Dearest Heavenly Father,

I thank You that I am not left to fight in my own strength. Today, I reject willpower and receive war power. Empower me through Your Spirit. Strengthen me through Your Word. Silence every lie of the enemy. I decree that I overcome by the blood of Jesus and the word of my testimony. I choose prayer, fasting, consecration, and Holy Spirit power. I take dominion over my thoughts, habits, and atmosphere. I will walk in victory every day. My name is Victory. In Jesus' Mighty Name, Amen.

12

I'M A NO NAME, COMING IN HIS NAME

"Therefore, God exalted Him to the highest place and gave Him the Name that is above every Name, that at the Name of Jesus every knee should bow, in heaven and on earth and under the earth, and every tongue acknowledge that Jesus Christ is Lord, to the glory of God the Father." - Philippians 2:9 to 11 NIV

There Is Power in the Name of Jesus

You do not need fame. You do not need a platform. You do not need the applause of people. As long as you are known in heaven, you carry influence.

You may be a NO NAME, but you carry THE NAME that holds all authority, all dominion, and all power, the Name of Jesus.

Bold Declaration: *I am a NO NAME, but I come in HIS NAME. His Name carries the full weight of heaven.*

You do not war in your own Name. You do not fight in your own strength. You pray in the Name that makes demons tremble and shakes the gates of hell. You pray in the Name that heaven responds to. You pray in the Name that hell fears.

> *"Whatever you ask in My Name, that will I do, that the Father may be glorified." - John 14:13*

The Name of Jesus breaks chains and destroys yokes. It shatters darkness. It activates angels. It silences demons and shifts atmospheres. It opens prison doors. It heals the sick. It restores what the enemy tried to steal.

Champions of Prayer do not seek to make a name for themselves. They exalt the Name above every Name, the Name of Jesus.

The Authority in His Name

> *"The seventy-two returned with joy and said, Lord, even the demons submit to us in Your Name. He replied, I saw Satan fall like lightning from heaven. I have given you authority." - Luke 10:17 to 19 NIV*

The disciples did not win spiritual battles because they were well-known. They won because they operated in the Name that causes hell to bow low, the Name of Jesus.

The word "submit" in this passage is the Greek word *hypotassō*. It means "to place under" or "to bring into submission." This means demons recognize that you carry the authority of heaven, and they must submit when you speak in the Name of Jesus.

Prophetic Charge:

Stop fighting for power. You already have it. Exercise your God given authority. Use the Name of Jesus and command the enemy to cease.

Champion Your Prayer Life Using His Name

Demons are subject to you through the authority of His Name. God has given you dominion. He has given you power to put your spiritual foot on the enemy and keep him there.

You do not have to tolerate spiritual harassment in your home, your mind, your workplace, or your children. Do not allow the enemy to influence your decisions or intimidate you with fear.

God has not given you a spirit of fear. He has given you the Spirit of power. What are you doing with that power? What are you saying with that authority?

"You cannot change what you tolerate."

Mike Murdock

Heaven will allow what you allow.

> *"Truly I tell you, whatever you bind on earth will be bound in heaven, and whatever you loose on earth will be loosed in heaven." - Matthew 18:18 NIV*

Champions of Prayer, raise the level of your warfare. Open your mouth and declare NO MORE. Whatever you say NO to, heaven backs. Whatever you say YES to, heaven establishes.

The power is in your decision. You must grab the horns of the altar and take back what the enemy has stolen.

Declaration:

In the Name of Jesus, I will champion my prayer life.

I will champion my faith.

I will champion my authority.

I will enforce my victory.

> Jesus said, *"Behold, I give you power... over all the power of the enemy. Luke 10:19*

This is not inspiration. This is delegation. This is dominion authority. This is warfare power.

Shut It Down in Jesus' Name

There is no name that carries the weight, wonder, and authority of His Name. No demonic power can withstand it. No stronghold can resist it. No situation is beyond its reach.

- At the Name of Jesus, demons tremble

- At the Name of Jesus, blind eyes open

- At the Name of Jesus, dead things come alive

- At the Name of Jesus, hell must surrender

Bold Declaration:

I am the church of the living God. I am filled with the Holy Spirit.

I come in the all-powerful Name of Jesus.

Stop allowing the devil to dominate. Rise in the authority of Jesus. Speak like you know who you are and whose you are. When you invoke His Name, heaven stands with you.

There is no name greater. There is no name stronger. There is no name with more power than the Name of Jesus.

Declare This Now: I Come in the Name of Jesus

• I am a NO NAME, coming in the Name of Jesus.

• I have power over the enemy through His Name.

• Demons submit to me because I use the authority of His Name.

• I walk in dominion, authority, and holy fire.

• I have a voice in heaven, and I shut down every demonic assignment through the Name of Jesus.

• I do not fight for victory. I fight from victory.

• The world may not know me, but heaven knows me.

• I am a Champion of Prayer, and I come in the Name above every Name. The Name of Jesus.

Prayer

Master, Savior, Jesus. I thank You for Your Name, the Name that is above every Name. I declare that I do not come in my own strength, title, or reputation. I come in the power of Your Name alone. Teach me to walk boldly in the authority You have given me. Empower me to pray in Your Name, fight in Your Name, take territory in Your Name, and tear down strongholds in Your

Name. I silence every lie of the enemy and step fully into my identity as a Champion of Prayer. No matter the attack, I will champion my faith, hold my ground, and call heaven to earth. In Your matchless, all-powerful Name, Jesus, I pray. Amen.

13

END-TIME CHURCH – THE BATTERING RAM

"He will direct the blows of his battering rams against your walls and demolish your towers with his weapons." - Ezekiel 26:9 NIV

Champions of Prayer Are Battering Rams in the Spirit

Intercessors. Champions of Prayer. You are God's battering ram, designed to break through walls, crush gates, and destroy the enemy's strongholds.

A battering ram was no ordinary tool of war. It was a deliberate, forceful, strategic weapon used to smash reinforced city gates and fortified walls. It did not strike once and stop. It struck again and again and again, until breakthrough came.

Declaration: *I am anointed to strike down every stronghold until the walls fall.*

Just like those ancient siege weapons, you are called to break resistance through persistence. Your prayers are not soft. Your faith is not weak. Your assignment is not optional. You are God's chosen weapon to demolish the enemy's defenses.

What Are Strongholds?

In nature, strongholds were castles, towers, and fortified walls.

In the Spirit, they are:

- Generational curses

- Demonic systems of oppression

- Mental fortresses of fear, shame, pride, and unbelief

- Cultural and ideological lies that resist truth

You are not called to avoid strongholds. You are called to target them, assault them, and demolish them through prayer, fasting, worship, and decrees.

Bold Statement: *Every stronghold must fall when a Champion of Prayer shows up.*

Designed for Breakthrough

God did not call you to be soft. You were not made to tap lightly on doors, you were forged to break them open.

> *"For the weapons of our warfare are not carnal, but mighty through God to the pulling down of strongholds." - 2 Corinthians 10:4*

The battering ram was purpose-built — heavy, focused, and effective. That is, you in the Spirit. You are not a random act of warfare. You are a divinely designed force of impact.

You have been:

- Called for this hour

- Anointed to pierce the darkness

- Equipped to confront strongholds

- Empowered to shift generations

Prophetic Declaration: *You are God's end-time plan to bring an all-out assault against the forces of darkness. You are a divine weapon of precision.*

Our Weapons Are Not of the Flesh

You do not need manmade tools. You carry the spiritual arsenal of heaven:

- The Sword of the Spirit

- The Shield of Faith

- The Name of Jesus

- The Power of the Blood

- The Authority of God's Word

These are the battering rams of the End-Time Church.

Bold Charge: *You have the power to shatter demonic deception, uproot darkness, and dismantle demonic strongholds.*

This is not a metaphorical war. It is spiritual. It is intense. It is now.

Declare This Now: I Am God's Battering Ram

- I am not weak. I am a spiritual weapon.

- I am a battering ram in the hands of God.

- I crush demonic strongholds.

- I tear down fortified lies.

- I press until a breakthrough happens.

- I demolish resistance with spiritual persistence.

- I am anointed for impact.

- I am a Champion of Prayer, and I was made for war.

Prayer: Make Me Your Battering Ram

Dearest Heavenly Father, I yield myself as Your instrument of breakthrough. Make me a battering ram in the Spirit — strategic, anointed, and unstoppable. I declare that I will not retreat. I will press forward until every wall falls. Use me to crush generational curses, dismantle demonic structures, and tear down lies. Fill me with boldness, wisdom, and power. Let me strike the gates of hell until revival bursts forth. I am not passive. I am available, forceful, and powerful, and I will fulfill my assignment. In Jesus' Mighty Name, Amen.

14

VOLUNTEERS IN THE DAY OF POWER

"Your people shall be volunteers in the day of Your power, in the beauties of holiness, from the womb of the morning, You have the dew of Your youth." - Psalm 110:3 NKJV

The Day of Power Is Now

This is God's hour of power, and He is calling for volunteers. You were born for this moment. You were set apart for this time. You have been chosen to be part of the greatest move of God the world has ever seen.

Bold Declaration: *I am a volunteer in the Day of His Power. I rise in strength, beauty, and holiness to fulfill my Kingdom assignment.*

God is not forcing anyone. He is looking for willing warriors, holy vessels who offer themselves freely and completely.

The Scripture says that this generation rises in the beauties of holiness from the womb of the morning. This speaks of fresh power, fresh oil, and a fresh beginning, just like the morning dew.

This is a spiritual awakening of the Armies of the Living God. We are refreshed, restored, and ready to invade darkness and advance the Kingdom of God in the earth.

The Demonstrative Power of God Shall Follow

"And these signs shall follow them that believe." Mark 16:17-18

Where is the move of God? The answer is simple. It is within you.

The time of empty talk is over. This is the season of demonstration.

God is raising a supernatural people who believe Him without limits. He will confirm His Word with signs that follow.

- Devils will flee

- The Holy Spirit will move with power

- Tongues from heaven will flow

- The sick will recover

- The dead will rise

- The Gospel will be demonstrated and not only declared

Prophetic Statement: *These signs shall accompany me because I believe in God.*

You are not only a believer.

You are an end-time demonstration of the power of the Living God.

Intercessors, we are on the frontlines. Hell wants to silence us because we bring heaven to earth through prayer. But hear this clearly.

God Is Fighting for You

"Let God arise, let His enemies be scattered..." — Psalm 68:1

You do not have to fear your enemies. God Himself is rising on your behalf, and when He rises, His enemies scatter.

Bold Charge: *God is not only for you. God is moving through you.*

Every demonic plan, every stronghold, and every weapon formed against you is being scattered, rerouted, and destroyed.

You Are God's Secret Weapon

"You are my battle ax and weapons of war." - Jeremiah 51:20

God is not raising passive spectators. He is raising militant warriors.

You are His battle ax. You are His instrument of justice, judgment, and breakthrough in the earth.

- You are God's militia

- You are anointed to carry out a prophetic purpose

- You are equipped to tear down

- You are built to advance

Prophetic Word: *You are God's battle ax. You were born for this war and anointed to win.*

Take Dominion Over Darkness

You are armed and dangerous in the Spirit. Rise and take dominion.

You carry the power of the Holy Ghost to confront demons and cancel:

- Every satanic resistance

- Every demonic demand

- Every generational limitation

- Every spiritual delay

- Every death assignment

- Every spell, incantation, and curse

Declaration: *By the Blood of Jesus, I uproot and overthrow every assignment of hell against my life, city, and nation.*

You were not born to survive the warfare.

You were born to lead the charge.

Activate your weapons of war. Pray. Intercede. Fast. Declare the Word. Plead the Blood of Jesus.

Plead the Blood of Jesus

Rhema: *The Blood is your banner, your defense, and your weapon.*

There is power in the Blood of Jesus to:

- Cancel accusations

- Overrule death wishes

- Silence the accuser

- Reverse demonic projections

- Dismantle demonic opposition

Bold Truth: *The Blood is speaking better things over your life. The Blood speaks victory, healing, purpose, and power.*

Declare This Now: I Am a Volunteer in the Day of God's Power

- I rise with the morning dew. I am refreshed, restored, and renewed

- I am God's weapon of war

- I wield the sword of the Spirit and release the fire of God

- I am covered in the Blood and clothed in power

- I plead the Blood against every spiritual attack

- I uproot every satanic assignment and destroy every stronghold

- I walk in divine power and Kingdom authority

- I am a Champion of Prayer, and I volunteer in the Day of His Power

Prayer: I Am a Volunteer in the Day of Power

Dearest Heavenly Father,

I am available. I volunteer. I report for duty on the Day of Your Power. I offer myself willingly, joyfully, and boldly. Use me as a vessel of holiness, fire, and authority. Make my life a demonstration of Your glory. Let signs and wonders follow me as I walk in obedience to Your call. I declare that no weapon formed against me shall prevail. Every enemy will scatter. I wield the sword of the Spirit and plead the Blood of Jesus over every battle. Empower me to carry out Your purpose and overturn every agenda of darkness, in Jesus' Mighty Name, Amen.

15

THE ARMY OF FIRE

"Then He spoke a parable to them that men always ought to pray and not lose heart." - Luke 18:1 NKJV

God Is Taking His Church Back

God is reclaiming His Church in this hour. He is not doing it through programs, personalities, or performances. He is doing it through the power of prayer.

He is calling the intercessors. He is waking the sleeping Church and drawing us back to our knees.

The Church was birthed in power with tongues of fire and the wind of the Spirit. The Church will also be taken home in power.

This is not a season to retreat. This is a season of revival.

Declaration: *I will be a praying believer. I will be part of the Church that walks in power.*

God is raising a people who will be the real Church—a Church marked by signs, wonders, and miracles. A Church the world cannot imitate. A Church that walks in spiritual authority. A Church that knows how to fight in prayer.

When God invites you to sit at the table of Champions, it means your season has arrived. It is time to become a Champion in your prayer life.

Prayer is not a burden. Prayer is your weapon, your access, and your power.

Persistent Prayer Brings Breakthrough

Jesus gave the parable of the persistent widow in Luke chapter 18. An unjust judge resisted her request, but she refused to stop asking. Her persistence broke through his resistance.

You must refuse to stop asking. You must refuse to give up. Your persistence will break through the resistance of hell.

If an unrighteous judge responds to persistence, how much more will your righteous and loving Father respond to the cries of His chosen ones? You are God's chosen one.

- You must always pray. Stay in a continual posture of prayer

- You must not faint. Do not lose heart. Do not stop. Stand in faith on God's promises

Bold Statement: *Persistent prayer is the language of faith.*

Delay does not mean denial. Heaven hears your cry. Press in and keep pressing.

While You Wait on God, Do Not Let the Enemy Derail Your Purpose

Spiritual warfare is real. The enemy tries to frustrate your timing, distract your focus, and disrupt your destiny.

But believers have the power and tools of God to stand firm and complete their assignments.

> *"For we are God's handiwork created in Christ Jesus to do good works which God prepared in advance for us to do." – Ephesians 2:10*

> *"Many are the plans in a person's heart, but it is the Lord's purpose that prevails." - Proverbs 19:21*

The plan of God for your life cannot be overruled by the enemy.

The enemy can only delay what you allow him to delay.

Bold Declaration: *Persistent prayer will shatter the power of delay and reveal purpose.*

Prophetic Charge: *God's purpose will prevail. My set time will not be delayed.*

Pray Until You See the Manifestation

Prayer is more than communication. Prayer is alignment, activation, and warfare.

Every persistent prayer builds faith, tears down resistance, and prepares you for manifestation.

God is not reluctant to answer you. He is aligning your heart so you can trust His timing.

Exercise your faith over your feelings. Prayer is powerful even when it is painful. Keep praying. Keep knocking. Keep standing.

Persistent prayer fueled by faith is a powerful way to approach God.

> *"Being confident of this, that He who began a good work in you will carry it on to completion until the day of Christ Jesus."* — *Philippians 1:6*

Declaration: *I will not faint. I will not quit. I will pray until the power of Heaven shows up.*

Persistent prayer empowers you to march in Kingdom power.

We Are the Remnant

We are the remnant God is raising to usher in the King of Glory.

This is not the hour to retreat. This is the hour to join the ranks.

Joel Chapter 2 Activation Charge — Join the Ranks

> *"Blow a trumpet in Zion. Sound an alarm on my holy mountain. Let all the inhabitants of the land tremble, for the day of the Lord is coming. It is near." - Joel chapter 2:1-11 ESV*

The Trumpet Is Sounding

The trumpet is sounding in Zion. This is not a soft call or whisper. It is a clear war cry from the throne of Heaven.

It is a summons to the end-time army of the Living God.

This is the hour for mobilization. No hesitation. Heaven's ranks are forming.

Those who hear the trumpet will not shrink back. They will rise. They will march. They will carry out the Word of the Lord.

Declaration: *I hear the trumpet. I rise at the sound of Heaven's call.*

The Army of Fire

The day of the Lord is near. Fire goes before His army, and a blazing flame follows behind.

This army is not lukewarm. This is a fire-forged and Spirit-filled people who leave no territory untouched and no gate unshaken.

> "Their appearance is like the appearance of horses, and like war horses, they run." – Joel 2:4

God's army is strong, disciplined, and unstoppable. They move with supernatural accuracy and spiritual precision.

They do not break ranks. They do not retreat. They move as one because they have been forged in the secret place of prayer.

They are not ordinary believers. They are Champions of Prayer. They are burning with holy fire and advancing with divine authority.

This army is not led by human strategy. It is led by the voice of the Lord who marches ahead of them.

Prophetic Word: *We are the Joel chapter 2 generation. We are a force of warriors who cannot and will not be silenced, shaken, or stopped.*

Unstoppable Warriors

> *"Like warriors, they charge. Like soldiers, they scale the wall. They march each on his way. They do not swerve from their paths." - Joel 2:7*

Every soldier in this army moves with divine assignment. They do not collide with one another. They work together to complete the mission.

They are unshakable. They break through enemy lines. They scale impossible walls. They tear down fortified gates. They occupy territories for the Kingdom of God.

Bold Declaration: *I will not retreat. I was born for this war.*

This army does not use earthly weapons. They are armed with

- The sword of the Spirit, which is the Word of God

- The power of the Blood of Jesus

- The fire of the Holy Ghost

- The authority of the Name of Jesus

- The unbreakable unity of the Spirit

Heaven's Earthquake

> *"The earth quakes before them. The heavens tremble. The sun and the moon grow dark, and the stars stop their shining." - Joel 2:10*

This is not a passive Church. This is a Kingdom invasion.

The presence of this end-time army shakes both the natural realm and the supernatural realm.

Demons tremble.

Systems collapse.

Strongholds shatter.

The heavens bear witness as the voice of God thunders through His people.

Rhema: *When the Joel chapter 2 army moves, hell steps back.*

We are the armies of the Living God. Heaven backs us, and hell fears us.

The King Himself leads His army.

The Voice of the Lord Thunders

"The Lord utters His voice before His army, for His camp is exceedingly great. The one who executes His word is powerful." - Joel 2:11

At the sound of His voice, every soldier moves. At the sound of His voice, angels respond.

At the sound of His voice, chains break. Revival fire sweeps across nations.

This army is not searching for attention. We are listening for orders.

And the Commander is speaking.

Prophetic Charge: *The Lord is calling His Joel chapter 2 army to arise. Will you join the ranks?*

This is the moment to take your place. No more delay. No more hesitation.

The voice of the Lord is thundering. Rise, Champion of Prayer, and take your position.

It is time to march forward in power.

Declare This Now: I Am a Joel 2 Warrior

- I hear the trumpet sounding, and I rise to the call

- I am part of the Joel chapter 2 army. I am unstoppable and unshakable

- I march in unity and I fight with heavenly weapons

- I follow the voice of the Lord

- I am forged for war, filled with the Spirit, and backed by Heaven

- My steps shake the earth, and my prayers shake the heavens

- The voice of the Lord thunders before me

- I am a Champion of Prayer, and I join the ranks of His end-time army

Prayer: Lord, Make Me a Warrior in Your Joel 2 Army

Father, I hear Your trumpet sounding and I respond to Your call. Make me a soldier in Your Joel chapter 2 army. Forge me in fire. Train me in prayer. Make my faith unshakable. I submit to Your voice, Your strategy, and your timing. Let holy fire burn behind me and divine authority go before me. Use me to shake nations, destroy strongholds, and advance Your Kingdom in the earth. I will not be silent. I will not stand idle. I join the ranks of Your mighty army. In Jesus' Mighty Name. Amen.

16

ARISE CHURCH. THE TIME IS NOW

"Arise, shine; for your light has come. And the glory of the Lord is risen upon you." - Isaiah 60:1 (NKJV)

This Is Heaven's Wake-Up Call

Church, the Spirit of the Lord is sounding the alarm. The trumpet is blowing. The time of spiritual slumber is over.

The Church of Jesus Christ is not called to hide. It is called to arise.

The Church is not called to simply survive. It is called to advance.

The Church is not called to blend in. It is called to stand out in boldness and power.

God did not give birth to a weak church. He gave birth to a powerful church. The season of a passive church is over.

The earth is groaning. Nations are trembling. Evil is raging. But the ekklesia, the called-out ones, the end-time remnant of God, is rising with fire, walking in fire, and calling down fire.

This is not just a call.

This is a command.

This is a prophetic summons from Heaven for the Church of the Living God to arise in glory, power, and Kingdom authority.

You were born for this moment.

History has been waiting for your arrival.

All creation is crying out, not for more religion, but for the revealing of the sons and daughters of God.

> "For the earnest expectation of the creature waits for the manifestation of the sons of God." - Romans 8:19 (KJV)

You have been enlisted. You have been equipped. You have been empowered. Now it is time to engage.

This is your time.

This is your hour.

This is your call to arise.

Arise in Power

We Are God's End Time Army

You were not called to be only a church member. You are a soldier in the army of the Living God.

You have been trained through trials.

You have been tested by fire.

You have been anointed for victory.

It is time to stop apologizing for your fire. You paid a price for that fire.

It is time to stop minimizing your anointing. The Holy Spirit equipped and empowered you to walk fully in the calling God placed within you.

You burn so that others can catch fire. It is time to shake off every lie of limitation and walk in the boldness of your Kingdom identity.

You are not a victim of this generation. You are a weapon in this generation.

Let the sleeping Church awaken.

Let the lukewarm be ignited.

Let the passive become prophetic.

Let the called become commissioned.

The Church is not weak. The Church becomes the greatest force on earth when fully awake.

Arise in the Spirit

The world does not need another program.

The world needs a Spirit-filled, Spirit-led, Spirit-empowered Church that knows how to pray, declare, and shift atmospheres.

You carry the Spirit of God.

You carry divine strategy.

You carry heavenly solutions.

You carry the glory.

When you arise, the glory of the Lord rises with you. And when the glory rises, darkness must bow.

Arise for the Nations

The Church is God's answer for this moment.

Jesus said these words:

> "Upon this rock I will build My Church, and the gates of hell shall not prevail against it." - Matthew 16:18

That is not a weak church.

That is a warring church.

That is a fire-baptized, Spirit-filled, world-shaking, devil-chasing, power-walking Church.

This is not only about your household.

This is not only about your personal breakthrough.

God is raising you for nations.

He is calling Champions of Prayer to do the following:

- Intercede on behalf of cities

- Speak prophetic direction over governments

- Fight for the destinies of generations

- Be a voice for the voiceless

- Declare the Word of the Lord to leaders, rulers, and kings

This is apostolic prayer.

This is governmental intercession.

This is the advancing Kingdom of God at war.

You are God's end-time specialist. You have been set apart for this very moment. We are not backing down. We are rising in power. We are not retreating. We are advancing with authority.

The Time Is Now

This is not the time to hesitate. Now is the time to pray.

This is not the time to be silent. Now is the time to raise your voice and declare the Word of life

This is not the time to shrink back. Now is the time to move out in power.

Now is the time to arise, to rule, to war, and to win.

> *"Arise, shine, for your light has come, and the glory of the Lord has risen upon you." - Isaiah 60:1*

Stop waiting for the perfect moment.

This is the moment.

Stop waiting for someone else to go first.

You are the answer to the cry of the earth.

Let every Champion of Prayer take their place in the secret place, on the wall, in the trenches, in the pulpit, and in the streets.

There is no Plan B. You are God's strategy.

Declare This Now

- I hear the call of God and I respond

- I arise in boldness, fire, and power

- I am part of the end-time move of God

- I walk in glory, speak with authority, and carry the fire of revival

- I am a Champion of Prayer, and I was born for such a time as this

Final Prayer: Lord, I Arise

Dearest Heavenly Father,

Awaken Your Church. Awaken your warriors. Awaken the fire inside me. Let the sleeping giants arise. Let the silent watchmen return to the wall. Use me to lead, to build, to intercede, and to take territory for the Kingdom.

I say yes to my assignment. I say yes to this moment.

I am a Champion of Prayer. I am a Champion of Faith. I am a battering ram. And I arise. I rise in prayer, in power, and in my prophetic purpose. Set me ablaze with fresh fire. Position me as a leader within this end-time army.

I yield to Your glory. I partner with Your Spirit. I decree that the Church is rising, and I take my place.

In Jesus' Mighty Name, Amen.

Closing Charge: Final Charge to the Champions of Prayer

> "But the people who know their God shall be strong and do exploits." - Daniel 11:32

You Have Been Trained. Now It Is Time to Fight

This is not simply the end of a book. This is the beginning of a movement.

You are now armed with truth, filled with fire, and charged by the Spirit of God to take your place on the battlefield of faith.

You are a Champion of Prayer.

You are a Warrior of the Word.

You are a Carrier of the Glory.

The world does not need more passivity. It needs your voice.

The Church does not need more spectators. It needs your strength.

Heaven is not looking for the qualified. Heaven is looking for the available.

Kingdom Commission

You have been called. You have been chosen. You have been trained. Now go.

Heaven Is Backing You

God told Jeremiah these words:

> *"Do not be afraid, for I am with you to deliver you," declares the Lord. - Jeremiah 1:8*

God is with you.

God is in you.

God is working through you.

No matter what the enemy attempts, the gates of hell will not prevail.

You were born for this hour.

You were raised for this generation.

You were fashioned in fire for a holy assignment.

Declaration

I will fight the good fight. I will finish my race. I will keep the faith. I will champion prayer. I will lead the charge.

From the Secret Place to the Frontlines

Let this book bring you to your knees and then send you into your destiny, your city, your family, and your nation.

Do not keep this fire to yourself. Set others on fire.

- Raise more Champions

- Equip intercessors

- Lead prayer movements

- Speak truth boldly

- Walk in power daily

You are the light in the darkness.

You are the trumpet in the silence.

You are the fire in the dry places.

This is your moment to champion. This is your moment to rise.

Arise. Pray. Declare. Lead. Win.

The Kingdom is counting on you.

APPENDIX: DECLARATIONS OF A CHAMPION AND PRAYERS

These declarations and prayers are spiritual weapons.

They are forged in the fire of intercession and anchored in the Word of God.

Speak them boldly. Decree them daily. Use them as spiritual weapons of war to enforce heaven's will on earth.

Chapter 1: Be an Army All by Yourself

Declaration

I am a one-person army with God. I will not wait. I will war. I take the Kingdom by force, and no power of darkness shall prevail against me.

Prayer

Lord, awaken the warrior in me. Help me stand even when I stand alone. Let me be a Champion who fights with faith and heaven's fire. In Jesus' Mighty Name, Amen.

Chapter 2: Champion Your Faith

Declaration

I am a Champion of Faith. I walk by what God says and not by what I see. I stand unshakable, unbreakable, and unstoppable in the face of every challenge.

Prayer

Lord, strengthen my faith. Let my belief in You burn brighter than any fear. Teach me to war in the Spirit and stand in truth. I am victorious in You. In Jesus' Mighty Name, Amen.

Chapter 3: Completely Surrender to the Holy Spirit

Declaration

I yield my heart, my mind, my will, and my body to the Holy Spirit. I surrender every thought, every plan, and every desire. I place everything under the dominion of God's Spirit. I no longer live by the cravings of my flesh. I walk by the Spirit, I live by the Spirit, and I war by the Spirit. I will not quench the Spirit. I will not grieve the Spirit. I will be led by the Spirit. I am governed, guided, and guarded by the breath of God. I am crucified with Christ. The life I now live is a Spirit-led life. I carry the fire of God in my bones. I obey without hesitation. I respond without resistance. I move without delay. I am a yielded vessel, a walking revival, and a carrier of God's power. I am surrendered, submitted, and set on fire. Speak through me. Burn in me. Flow through me. Use me for Your glory. In Jesus' Mighty Name, Amen.

Prayer

Lord, I thank You for the gift of faith. Today, I take my place as a Champion of Faith. I choose to believe Your Word, walk in Your ways, and live by the power of Your Spirit. Strengthen me in the face of adversity and make me bold in my convictions. Let my life be a testimony to Your unfailing power and love. In Jesus' Mighty Name, Amen.

Chapter 4: Will You Join the Ranks

Declaration

My name belongs in the Hall of Faith. I walk in radical obedience. I live by faith. I speak by faith. I leave a legacy of faith.

Prayer

Lord, let my life be worthy of remembrance in heaven. Let my faith echo for generations. Use my obedience to shake nations. I do not want safe faith. I want bold and mountain-moving faith. I declare today that I will not shrink back. I will live boldly. I will trust radically. I will believe faithfully. I am a Champion of Faith. Count me among those who will Join the Ranks. In Jesus' Mighty Name, Amen.

Chapter 5: Prayer Warrior's Activation

Declaration

I am a prayer warrior. My prayers are fire. My intercession changes nations. I war in the Spirit and pull down every stronghold.

Prayer

Lord, train me in the school of prayer. Teach me to pray like Jesus with power, passion, and purpose. Give me eyes to see, ears to hear, and boldness to declare Your Word. Empower me to stand in the gap for my family, my church, my city, and my nation. I take my post. I sound the alarm. Let my prayers cause heaven to move and let hell tremble. Let my prayers birth revival and destroy the works of darkness. In Jesus' Mighty Name, Amen.

Chapter 6: A Cry for Revival

Declaration

I am a move of God. I carry fire. I release revival. I declare that heaven is invading earth through me.

Prayer

Lord, we cry out for a move of Your Spirit in our generation. Not only the revivals of the past but a present-day outpouring that touches every heart, every home, and every city. Shake everything that can be shaken. Burn everything that must be burned. Awaken what has been sleeping. Use us to bring heaven to earth. We are available and yield. Let revival begin in me. Let it sweep across the world. Use my life, my words, and my prayers to set this generation ablaze with Your fire. In Jesus' Mighty Name, Amen.

Chapter 7: Prayer for Spiritual Boldness

Declaration

I rise in boldness. I am called to lead and anointed to win. I will not shrink back. I rise in confidence and Holy Ghost authority.

Prayer

Lord, I surrender to Your call, and I am available to lead. I reject fear and embrace the oil You have placed on my life. Give me boldness like David, discernment like Deborah, and unwavering trust like Daniel. I refuse to shrink back. I rise to lead. Let the power of Your Holy Spirit flow through me. Empower me to speak truth, wage war in prayer, and walk in victory. In Jesus' Mighty Name, Amen.

Chapter 8: Intercessor's Cry

Declaration

I am a spiritual gatekeeper. I stand in the gap. I intercede with power. No weapon formed against my family, my church, or my city will prosper.

Prayer

Lord, awaken the watchman in me. Train my hands for war and my heart for intercession. Make me alert in the Spirit. Make me a gap stander and a burden bearer. Let me see what you see and feel what you feel. Break my heart with what breaks Yours. I take my place in prayer with fire in my spirit and authority in my voice. Use my intercession to protect, restore, and release Your glory in the earth. May revival be birthed through my obedience. In Jesus' Mighty Name, Amen.

Chapter 9: Declaration of Dominion Authority

Declaration: My Words Create and Activate

My words create, activate, and release. I speak life. I decree truth. I declare a breakthrough.

Prayer

Lord, help me to guard my mouth and speak with authority. Train me to prophesy, decree, and speak only what aligns with Your Word. In Jesus' Mighty Name, Amen.

Declaration

I decree and declare:

- I am seated with Christ in heavenly places.

- I uproot every stronghold by the authority of God's Word.

- I speak life over my family, city, and nation.

- I walk in divine power and kingdom purpose.

- No weapon formed against me or those connected to me shall prosper.

Chapter 10: Releasing Dominion in Prayer

Declaration: I Am Positioned in Power

I am seated together with Christ in heavenly places. I pray from a position of power and victory. I walk in dominion. I enforce heaven's agenda on the earth.

Prayer

Lord, teach me to pray from the throne room. I thank You that through Christ, I have been seated in heavenly places. I operate through the mantle of dominion authority. Teach me to pray with power, to speak with authority, and to war with boldness. Let my intercession shift the winds of adversity, reestablish order in governments, shape nations, influence atmospheres, and bring the power of heaven to earth. I declare I am a victor. I walk in dominion. I pray from the place of power. Let every word I pray be backed by the weight of Your glory. In Jesus' Mighty Name, Amen.

Chapter 11: I Choose War Power Over Willpower

Declaration: I Am Empowered by the Spirit. No Spirit No Power

- I do not fight in my flesh. I fight in the Spirit.

- I live from war power, not willpower.

- I fast. I pray. I decree. I dominate.

- I silence every lie. I shut down every scheme.

- I am clothed in power and led by the Spirit.

- Temptation cannot hold me. Truth has freed me.

- I am more than a conqueror through Christ.

- I am a Champion of Prayer, and I walk in Holy Ghost war power.

Prayer

Lord, today I declare that I no longer rely on my strength. I choose spiritual war power over human willpower. I connect to You daily through prayer, fasting, and the Word. I activate every spiritual weapon You have given me. I decree that temptation is broken, strongholds are destroyed, and fear is defeated, not by might and not by power, but by Your Spirit. Fill me with fresh fire. Equip me to win. Let heaven fight on my behalf as I take my position in the Spirit. I war from a place of victory. In Jesus' Mighty Name, Amen.

Chapter 12: I Come in the Name of Jesus

Declaration: I Am a No Name Coming in His Name

- I do not need a title. I have the Name of Jesus.

- Demons are subject to me through His authority.

- I shut down demonic activity with heaven's backing.

- I speak boldly because I carry the name.

- I am not famous in the world. I am known in heaven.

- My prayers are weapons. My words carry fire.

- I trample on serpents and scorpions.

- I am a Champion of Prayer and I come in the Name of Jesus.

Prayer

Lord Jesus, I thank You that my authority does not come from my name, but from Yours. I come in the name that is above every name, Jesus. Let every demon flee, every wall fall, and every chain break when I call on Your Name. Help me to walk boldly, live faithfully, and pray with authority. I take dominion over every demonic assignment and declare that Your Name is power, freedom, healing, and victory. Use me as a vessel of deliverance, fire, and glory, all in the power of Your Name. Jesus, Amen.

Chapter 13: Prayer: Use Me as a Battering Ram

Declaration: I Was Created for This

- I am not afraid of strongholds. I was made to destroy them.

- I do not retreat. I advance.

- I am not gentle with darkness. I strike with authority.

- My prayers are battering rams.

- My decrees shatter gates.

- My worship opens portals.

- My persistence breaks resistance.

- I am the End Time Church. I am the Battering Ram of God.

Prayer

Lord, use me as a battering ram in the Spirit. I surrender to Your strategy and yield to Your command. Let my prayers strike the gates of darkness and tear down every stronghold. I press, I push, and I persist until a breakthrough comes. Every wall the enemy built must fall. Every gate of resistance must be breached. Make me unshakable, unbreakable, and unstoppable in Your hands. In Jesus' Mighty Name, Amen.

Chapter 14: I Report for Duty

Declaration: I Am the Move of God

- I am a sign on the earth.

- I am a holy volunteer in the Day of Power.

- I carry the dew of the morning and the fire of the Spirit.

- I am armed with truth, soaked in oil, and covered in the Blood.

- No fear, no demon, and no delay can stop me.

- I silence the voice of accusation and rise in victory.

- I am a Champion of Prayer, and I am the move of God.

Prayer

Lord, I report for duty in the Day of Your Power. I am not waiting. I am rising. Empower me to confront darkness with boldness and take back territory for Your Kingdom. I plead the Blood of Jesus over my life, family, ministry, and assignment. I silence the accuser and cancel every demonic plot. Make me your battle ax. Use me as a sign and a wonder. I will not hold back. I will not be silent. I will not shrink. I am ready. I am willing. I am anointed. In Jesus' Mighty Name, Amen.

Chapter 15: I Am a Champion of Prayer

- I pray without ceasing.

- I refuse to faint.

- I walk in divine timing.

- I am aligned with the will of God.

- I overcome delay, distraction, and discouragement.

- My prayers break resistance.

- My words shake strongholds.

- My faith cannot be silenced.

- My prayer life is a weapon of power in the hands of a holy God.

- I will see the manifestation of His power.

- I stand in the gap for my generation.

- I am a Champion of Prayer, and I will not quit.

Prayer: Lord, Ignite My Prayer Life

Father, today I choose to champion my prayer life. Take me deeper, higher, and stronger in intercession. Teach me to pray without ceasing and to stand without fainting. Lord, I bind the spirit of fainting and loose the spirit of persistence. I will pray through every battle, every delay, and every storm. Align my heart with Your timing. Ignite my heart with holy fire. Let my prayers shake the heavens and shift the earth. I break every assignment of delay, distraction, and discouragement. I declare that my prayer life will be a furnace of fire. Use me as a weapon in Your hand to shift atmospheres, release revival, and usher in Your glory. My faith will not fail. I will not quit. My voice will not be silenced. I will pray until I see Your power manifest. In Jesus' Mighty Name, Amen.

Chapter 16: The Army Is Rising

Declaration: I Carry the Glory

I hear the sound of the trumpets. I hear the call of the Spirit, and I arise. I am part of God's end-time army. I carry glory, walk in fire, start fires, and war in victory.

Prayer

Lord, awaken Your Church. Awaken your warriors. Awaken the fire inside of me. Let the slumbering giants arise. Let the sleeping watchmen return to the wall. I arise. I will not delay. I take my place as a Champion of Prayer. Use me to ignite the Church, confront darkness, and release revival fires to the nations. I am a Champion of Prayer, and I will arise. In Jesus' Mighty Name, Amen.

CONCLUSION

THIS IS A CALL TO CHAMPION YOUR PRAYER LIFE

"...but the people who know their God shall stand firm and take action."- Daniel 11:32 ESV

Beloved Champion, hear the word of the Lord. This is the hour to rise. This is the hour to pray. This is the hour to walk in the power of God and take action. Heaven is not looking for observers. Heaven is looking for warriors.

There is an urgency in the Spirit. A divine stirring. A call that is moving across the earth.

"My people must return to the altar."

Prayer is not simply a discipline. It is your lifeline, your weapon, your mantle, and your mandate.

A prayerless believer is a powerless believer.

A believer who prays with fire is uncontainable.

A believer who prays with authority is undeniable.

A believer who prays with persistence is unstoppable.

Today, God is calling you to step fully into your identity as a Champion of Prayer.

Rise and Take Your Rank in Heaven's Spiritual Militia

The time for hesitation is over.

The time for silence is over.

The time for passive Christianity is over.

You are part of the end-time Church, the army of the Living God, appointed to shake nations.

Your voice matters in Heaven.

Your prayers shift atmospheres.

Your declarations dismantle darkness.

Your intercession brings Heaven to earth.

You are God's battering ram in the Spirit.

You are God's war trumpet in the earth.

You are God's battle ax and weapon of war.

When you pray, demons scatter. Strongholds crumble. Angels are released. The will of God invades the earth.

Prayer Is Your Place of Power

Every time you pray

You choose victory over defeat

You choose faith over fear

You choose destiny over delay

You choose divine intervention over human limitation

Your prayer life is not small.

Your prayer life is not insignificant.

Your prayer life is not optional.

Your prayer life is your life of power.

Your prayer life is your life of faith.

Your prayer life is your life of victory.

Champions of Prayer do not wait for things to change. We make things change.

We legislate in the Spirit.

We speak God's Word.

We fight with Heaven's weapons.

We partner with the Holy Spirit until breakthrough becomes reality.

We Are the Church God Is Raising Up

God is restoring the praying Church

The Church of fire

The Church of power

The Church of miracles

The Church of dominion

The Church that storms the gates of hell and wins

The Church Heaven recognizes

The Church hell fears

The Church the world cannot ignore

That Church is you.

FINAL PROPHETIC ACTIVATION

Place your hand on your heart and declare with holy authority

"Today, I rise as a Champion of Prayer.

I will pray until Heaven moves.

I will speak until chains break.

I will intercede until mountains fall.

I will stand in my authority.

I will fight in the Spirit.

I will not faint. I will pray.

I will not retreat. I will advance.

I am a Champion of Prayer.

I am a Champion of Faith.

I will fulfill my Kingdom assignment

through the power of the Holy Spirit.

In the mighty Name of Jesus, Amen."

www.ingramcontent.com/pod-product-compliance
Lightning Source LLC
Chambersburg PA
CBHW050648160426
43194CB00010B/1853